I0012281

AI for Beginners Made Easy

A guide for beginners

Epris E. Ezekiel

Contents

Introduction

Upskilling is the only way to stay current in an AI-driven environment, and those who can adapt and use new technologies will do well in the future employment market. Recent technology breakthroughs have fueled enthusiasm about the potential and anxiety of becoming obsolete. While businesses' embrace of artificial intelligence has led to the automation of many activities, new positions continue to emerge daily.

The importance of artificial intelligence (AI) is growing, with 97% of business owners expecting ChatGPT to improve their operations.

But how can you learn AI from scratch? Which abilities will stand the test of time and remain relevant in today's dynamic workplace?

This book will assist you in navigating the vast ocean of knowledge and developing a comprehensive learning plan. We'll look at the fundamentals of artificial intelligence, its numerous varieties, in-demand abilities, and the critical concepts you must understand. We will also provide you with a variety of useful materials to help you get started.

Chapter 1

What is AI (Artificial Intelligence)?

Artificial intelligence (AI) is a computer science area that focuses on developing systems capable of executing activities that would normally require human intelligence, such as comprehending natural language, identifying patterns, making decisions, and learning through experience. AI is a large field with several subfields, each with its own set of goals and specializations, and it is distinct from machine learning, which will be discussed separately.

Types of AI

As AI gains prominence, it is discussed in a variety of ways. To simplify the remainder of the essay, consider the various types of AI.

AI can be classified into three tiers based on its capabilities:

Artificial Super Intelligence (ASI): The ultimate level of AI, ASI, refers to a future situation in which AI outperforms human intelligence in almost all economically valuable tasks. This hypothesis, while intriguing, is mostly hypothetical.

Artificial Narrow Intelligence (ANI): This is the most frequent type of AI we encounter today. ANI is intended to execute a specific task, such as voice recognition or suggestions for streaming services.

Artificial General Intelligence (AGI): An AI with AGI can understand, learn, adapt, and apply knowledge to a wide range of human-level tasks. While huge language models and tools like ChatGPT have demonstrated the potential to generalize across multiple activities, as of 2024, this is still a theoretical idea.

Despite how advanced current breakthroughs appear to be, we are still in the early stages of weak AI. Super intelligent AI is a fictitious idea; only time will tell if humanity will reach that level. Nonetheless, we're closer than ever to AGI. What a wonderful moment to study AI!

The distinction between data science, artificial intelligence, machine learning, and deep learning.

Topic	Artificial Intelligence	Machine Learning	Deep Learning	Big Data	Data Science
Definition	The concept of creating intelligent machines is known as artificial	A computer science subject that employs computer algorithms and analytics to develop forecast	Deep learning is a branch of machine learning that uses algorithms built after the	A method of gathering, conserving, and processing massive amounts of data.	It is a field that involves obtaining, managing, evaluating, and combini

	intelligence.	ing models.	human brain's structures and operations.		ng data into various procedures.
Types	Reactive machine with limited memory, theory of mind, and self-awarenes	Supervised, semi-supervised, unsupervised, and reinforced	convolutional neural networks, recurrent neural networks, generative adver	Data might be structured, unstructured, or semi-structured.	N/A

	s		sarial networks, and deep belief networks		
Application	Self-driving cars, AI robots, Apple Siri, or Google Assistant	Sales forecasting, fraud detection, and product recommendations.	Music creation, cancel tumor identification, and object retention.	Create a learning management system and recommend content on dema	Speech recognition, advanced picture recognition, and flight path plan

				nd.	ning

Chapter 2

Why Should I Learn Artificial Intelligence Right Now?

Artificial intelligence (AI) is a disruptive technology that is changing our lives and careers. With the growing demand for AI abilities due to the explosion of data, now is the ideal moment to begin learning AI.

- ❖ **AI presents intellectual challenges.** Artificial intelligence is about more than simply high-paying professions and market demand; it also provides intellectual stimulation through complicated problem-solving algorithms, human intelligence simulation models, and innovative technology applications in real-world scenarios.

AI professionals are always learning, adapting, and innovating, creating a dynamic environment for people who thrive on challenges and continual learning. The field is continually changing, presenting new difficulties and chances for growth.

❖ AI is a high-paying job.

The growing demand for AI capabilities has resulted in more appealing compensation, with the average annual income for an AI engineer in the United States being $128,479, with potential incentives and profit sharing. Machine learning and data scientists earn comparable wages, demonstrating the market worth and effect of AI expertise.

❖ AI is a rapidly expanding field.

The World Economic Forum's Future of Jobs report identifies AI and machine learning professionals as the fastest-growing jobs over the next five years. As enterprises use AI to streamline operations and make smarter decisions, the demand for AI specialists is projected to rise.

Applications of AI

Artificial intelligence is now an important component of our daily life. AI applications exist in a variety of industries, including healthcare, finance, education, and e-commerce. If you're interested in learning AI, you should consider how it could help you with your current job. The following are how artificial intelligence is influencing several industries.

Artificial intelligence in social media

- ✓ **Sentiment Analysis:** Artificial intelligence employs sentiment analysis to find trends by examining large amounts of text data. It aids in determining public opinion on a variety of topics, giving useful information for businesses and scholars. AI also monitors and controls online reputation, allowing businesses to respond to client complaints more effectively.
- ✓ **Material Recommendation:** AI systems analyze user behavior to suggest appropriate material, which increases user engagement. These algorithms are becoming more intelligent, analyzing the intricacies of user behavior and making more accurate

recommendations.

The varied range of AI applications highlights its critical role in influencing the future of our society and economy.

AI for Marketing

- ✓ **Predictive Analysis:** AI assists in identifying potential customers and optimizing ad targeting. It uses massive volumes of data to forecast client behavior, allowing firms to reach the right audience at the right moment. Furthermore, artificial intelligence anticipates future sales patterns, allowing businesses to better plan their marketing tactics.
- ✓ **Personalization:** AI tailors online marketing campaigns to individual clients, creating a more personalized experience that boosts engagement and conversion rates. AI automates email marketing efforts, sending clients personalized emails based on their behavior and preferences.

AI in transportation.

- ✓ **Ride-sharing services:** Companies such as Uber and Lyft utilize predictive analytics to forecast demand and alter costs based on distance, time, and destination. AI also pairs riders with drivers in a timely and efficient manner.
- ✓ **Self-driving vehicles:** AI is at the heart of self-driving cars, managing navigation, traffic, and collision avoidance. This technology has the potential to transform transportation by improving safety and efficiency. AI also optimizes real-time routes based on traffic data, resulting in faster travel times.

AI in finance.

- ✓ **Market analysis:** AI systems examine

historical data to identify market patterns, which helps firms make decisions. They help with financial planning and forecasting, resulting in lucrative business decisions. Furthermore, AI is used to make real-time trading decisions in stock markets by exploiting its predictive capabilities.

- ✓ **Fraud detection:** AI systems use patterns and trends to identify fraudulent transactions. This proactive technique reduces theft and ensures the security of financial transactions. AI predicts future frauds based on historical data, which strengthens security measures.

AI in education.

- ✓ **Gamification:** AI enables gamification in education. E-learning organizations increasingly create interactive learning games to further involve students in the learning process. Furthermore, AI generates adaptive learning paths, making learning more engaging and effective.
- ✓ **Personalized learning:** Among the educational AI applications are tailored services and experiences for students based on their learning goals. This strategy ensures that each student receives the attention and assistance they require to succeed. AI may also identify learning gaps and provide corrective actions to improve student performance.

AI in E-Commerce

- ✓ **Customer support:** AI-powered chatbots respond to customer requests around the clock, dramatically improving customer service. These chatbots can answer common questions, deliver information, and even facilitate transactions. They are designed to interpret conversational language, making consumer interactions more human-like.
- ✓ **Personalized suggestions:** AI makes exact recommendations to clients based on their search history and interests. These AI recommendation models improve the online shopping experience by proposing things that the user might like. Additionally, AI predicts future purchasing patterns, allowing firms to better manage their inventory.

AI and Healthcare

- ✓ **Medical imaging:** AI research has made major contributions to medical imaging, assisting physicians and radiologists in diagnosing various illnesses. AI algorithms may evaluate photos to identify potential areas of concern, hence improving diagnostic accuracy and efficiency. AI in healthcare can also detect early indicators of diseases like cancer, which improves patient outcomes.

✓ **Predictive models:** AI uses predictive models to forecast patient outcomes and diagnose ailments. These models examine a large number of data points to predict potential health hazards, allowing for early interventions. Furthermore, with the advent of AI, it is now able to forecast the spread of infectious diseases and manage public health crises more effectively.

Chapter 3

How to learn AI from scratch

Learning AI necessitates a clear plan, adequate resources, and a deliberate approach. Despite its vast scope and countless subtopics, it can be effectively accessed with the correct tools.

Develop specialized AI skills.
AI is a fast-expanding profession that necessitates a thorough understanding of a variety of skills, which can be acquired through a variety of qualifications depending on the exact job in which one intends to succeed.

1. Statistics
Statistics is a critical field that collects, organizes, analyzes, interprets, and presents data. It serves as the foundation for understanding AI and managing data.

✓ The Introduction to Statistics Course includes measurements of center and spread, probability distributions, and hypothesis testing. The Introduction to

Statistics in R course covers variables, graphing, and standard deviation in R.

✓ The Statistics Fundamentals with Python Skill Track teaches four core statistics in Python: summary statistics, probability, linear and logistic regression models, sampling approaches, hypothesis testing, and data set conclusions.

2. Mathematics

AI algorithms rely on mathematical tools such as linear algebra, calculus, probability, and differential equations, all of which are necessary for AI development.

- ✓ Covers random variables, including mean and variance.
- ✓ Foundations of Probability in Python
- ✓ Fundamentals of linear algebra, including matrix-vector equations, eigenvalue/eigenvector analysis, and PCA.
- ✓ Linear Algebra for Data Science with R
- ✓ Deciphering Mathematical Concepts for Deep Learning

3. Programming

Understanding programming is essential for AI implementation since it enables the creation of algorithms, data manipulation, and the use of AI tools and libraries.

Python is the most popular programming language due to its simplicity, flexibility, and abundance of data science packages.

Python Programming Skills Track

- ✓ Encourages code optimization and function writing.
- ✓ Improves R programming skills.
- ✓ Learns to use popular data structures.

4. Data Structures

Understanding data structures such as arrays, trees, lists, and queues is essential for creating efficient code and complicated AI algorithms. The Introduction to Data Structures and Algorithms Course covers a wide range of Python data structures, such as linked lists, stacks, queues, hash tables, and graphs, while the Python Data Structures with Primitive & Non-Primitive Examples Tutorial teaches data types.

5. Data Science

Data science is a collection of tools, algorithms, and machine learning methods designed to uncover hidden patterns in raw data. As an AI practitioner, you must grasp how to extract insights from data.

- ✓ The Data Science program provides a thorough understanding of data science and its usefulness.
- ✓ The Data Scientist with Python Career Track concentrates on Python skills, whereas the Data Scientist with R Career Track emphasizes R programming skills.

6. Data manipulation

Data manipulation entails cleaning, transforming, and manipulating data for analysis or AI models, which necessitates proficiency in libraries such as pandas.

- ✓ **Pandas:** Use Data Frames to extract, filter, and transform real-world datasets.
- ✓ **Python:** Transform, sort, and filter data in Data Frames to facilitate analysis.
- ✓ **R:** Describes the similar approach in the R programming language.

Chapter 4

Challenges in Artificial Intelligence

Artificial intelligence (AI) is leading the way in innovation, bringing significant advances to various fields. However, despite all of the great prospects, AI confronts some significant challenges.

In this essay, we will look at the top AI difficulties. From technical challenges to ethical considerations, we'll look at the obstacles that AI must overcome to reach its full potential.

This reading discusses some of these issues and how businesses might overcome them to adopt AI in their work culture. So, let's look at these issues immediately!

Social and Economic Challenges of AI

These challenges focus on the broader societal consequences of AI:

1. **Need for new regulations**
   - ✓ As AI gets more advanced, we must create new legislation and policies to control its development and

use. These rules may address concerns such as bias, privacy, and safety.

✓ For example, regulations governing how AI can be used in facial recognition software to ensure that people's privacy is not violated.

2. **Impact on jobs**

   ✓ AI automation is projected to replace many tasks currently performed by humans, perhaps causing widespread unemployment and economic disruptions.

   ✓ For example, automation in manufacturing may result in employment losses among assembly line workers.

3. **Widening Inequality**

   ✓ Access to AI may exacerbate existing social and economic inequities. others who have access to advanced AI technology may grow even more powerful, while others who do not may fall behind.

✓ For example, wealthy organizations may use AI to increase automation and profits, while smaller enterprises struggle to keep up.

Ethical Considerations for AI

These challenges center on the ethical aspects of developing and applying AI:

1. **Potential for Malicious Use.**

    ✓ AI could be utilized for malevolent reasons. Consider autonomous weapons that operate without human intervention, or deep fakes deployed to spread misinformation and propaganda.

    ✓ For example, creating AI systems capable of hacking key infrastructure or manipulating financial markets for personal benefit.

2. **Bias**

  ✓ AI systems might inherit biases from the data on which they are taught. If the training data is skewed, the AI's outputs are likely to reflect this bias. This can lead to discriminatory outcomes, such as an AI loan approval system that favors specific populations.

  ✓ For example, an AI system trained on a collection of news items featuring predominantly males in leadership posts may be more likely to recommend men for future leadership positions.

3. **Transparency and accountability**

  ✓ It can be difficult to grasp how complex AI systems make judgments. This lack of transparency makes it harder to hold them responsible for any undesirable results.

✓ For example, an AI system used in criminal justice may refuse someone parole based on complex computations, but the reasoning behind that decision may be opaque, impeding any appeals procedure.

Technical Challenges in AI

These challenges address the technical obstacles we confront when constructing powerful AI systems:

1. **Interoperability**
   ✓ There are no uniform standards for AI development. Data and model formats or structures may vary across AI systems. This makes it harder to share data and work with other AI systems.

   ✓ Consider an AI healthcare system produced by one business that is incompatible with another's system, preventing the sharing of patient data for better diagnosis.

2. **Handling Complex Tasks.**
   - ✓ Current AI struggles with tasks that require commonsense understanding. Consider an AI attempting to interpret a joke or manage a busy sidewalk. These circumstances entail real-world complications that AI algorithms are typically unable to handle.

   - ✓ For example, a self-driving car may encounter an unforeseen impediment, such as a child playing on the street. The car may struggle to react effectively if it does not understand the intricacies of the situation.

3. **Scalability and Efficiency**
   - ✓ Training powerful AI models frequently necessitates vast amounts of data and computational resources. This can be costly and time-consuming, making it challenging to implement AI solutions in real-world settings.

✓ For example, training a big language model like mine on a massive dataset of text and code necessitates a significant amount of computer power, which might be prohibitively expensive for small businesses or academic organizations.

Chapter 5

What Are the Most Difficult Obstacles to Implementing AI?

1. **Cost requirements**

   Based on what we've talked about thus far, it's clear that developing, implementing, and incorporating Artificial Intelligence into your training approach will not be inexpensive. To get it properly, you'll need to work with AI professionals who have the requisite expertise and abilities, implement an ongoing AI training program for your personnel, and most likely update your IT infrastructure to meet the demands of your machine learning tools. Although it is impossible to eliminate some of these expenses, you can reduce them by researching low-cost training programs or free applications. There are several solutions available to help you determine which AI capabilities your training program will benefit from before investing money in them.

2. **Overestimate Your AI System**

   The technical developments we've seen sometimes lead us to feel that technology can't do anything bad. However, AI is dependent on the data it provides, and if that data is incorrect, the conclusions it makes will be flawed. A significant issue in AI implementation is the complexity of the learning process, particularly when attempting to structure it into a set of data that can be imported into a system. For this reason, AI explainability is critical for a smooth transition to machine learning. Breaking down algorithms and instructing people on the decision-making process of Artificial Intelligence increases transparency and helps to avoid improper operations.

3. **Lack of AI Talent**

   While we're on the issue of expertise, given how new the concept of AI in learning and education is, it's fair to argue that finding people with the appropriate knowledge and abilities is a significant challenge. Many firms avoid experimenting with artificial intelligence due to a lack of internal knowledge. Although looking for a vendor to help your firm migrate to machine learning is a realistic option, forward-thinking businesses are deciding that investing in their internal knowledge base is more helpful in the long term. In other words, they recommend training your personnel in AI development and deployment, employing AI experts, and even licensing capabilities from other IT organizations to construct learning prototypes internally.

4. **Integration with Existing Systems** Incorporating AI into your training program entails much more than simply installing a few plugins for your LMS. As previously indicated, you must take the time to determine whether you have the storage, processors, and infrastructure required for the system to perform properly. At the same time, your personnel must be trained to use their new tools, fix minor issues, and identify

when the AI algorithm is underperforming. Collaborating with a provider with the requisite AI knowledge and skills will help you overcome all of these challenges and ensure the smoothest transition to machine learning possible.

5. **Outdated infrastructure.**
To get the required results, Artificial Intelligence systems must process vast amounts of data in fractions of a second. The only way to accomplish this is to run on devices with appropriate infrastructure and computing power. However, many firms continue to use old equipment that is incapable of meeting the challenges of AI deployment. Businesses that want to use machine learning to change their learning and development techniques must be prepared to invest in cutting-edge infrastructure, tools, and applications.

6. **Insufficient or low-quality data.** AI systems are trained on a set of data that is relevant to the problem at hand. However, corporations frequently struggle to "feed" their AI algorithms with the appropriate quality or volume of data, either because they lack access to it or because the quantity does not yet exist. This imbalance can result in inconsistent or even discriminating results when using your AI system. This issue, also known as the bias problem, can be avoided if you use representative and high-quality data. Furthermore, it is ideal to begin your AI journey with simpler algorithms that you can simply understand, test for bias, and alter as needed.

Chapter 6

How to Create Your AI System in 7 Simple Steps

Gartner predicts strong growth in the AI sector, with a compound annual growth rate (CAGR) of 36.6% between 2024 and 2030. This expansion indicates ongoing innovation and greater acceptance of advanced technology across a variety of industries. This spike demonstrates AI's growing importance in improving operational efficiencies and developing new market opportunities for businesses worldwide.

So, how do you create an AI? Let's walk through the fundamental procedures to assist you learn how to build an AI from the start.

Step 1: Determine the problem you want to solve with AI. Define Your Objective.
Begin by establishing your goals. Ask yourself, "What specific problem will AI solve?" For example, using an AI scheduling system in healthcare could reduce patient wait times.

When defining your aim, identify measurable benchmarks, such as reducing patient wait times by 20% or 30%. Clear metrics assist guides the development process and assess the AI system's success.

To successfully identify the problem, you must examine and comprehend the current system challenges by examining patient flow data and peak hours. Keep track of your findings so you can explain the goal and approach to all stakeholders.

Step 2: Gather and prepare the data. Now that you've defined the problem, you need to select the appropriate data sources. It is more important to collect high-quality data than to spend time enhancing the AI model itself. Data falls into two categories:

✓ Structured Data

Structured data is well-defined information that incorporates patterns and searchable parameters. Examples include names, addresses, birth dates, and phone numbers.

✓ Unstructured data.

Unstructured data lacks patterns, consistency, and homogeneity. It contains audio, photos, infographics, and emails.

Next, you must clean, process, and store the cleansed data before using it to train the AI model. Data cleaning or cleansing is the process of removing errors and omissions to improve the quality of data.

Step 3: Select a programming language. There are other programming languages, including the classic C++, Java, Python, and R. The latter two coding languages are more popular because they provide a comprehensive set of tools, including significant machine-learning libraries. Consider your goals and needs before making a decision. For example:

✓ R is designed for predictive analysis and statistics. So, it's largely employed in data science.

✓ Java is simple to debug, user-friendly, and can be run on a variety of systems. Furthermore, it works well with search engine algorithms and on large-scale projects. Typically, Java is used to create desktop apps.

✓ Python is an excellent choice for novices since it has the simplest syntax that a non-programmer may quickly grasp.

✓ C++ has tremendous performance and efficiency, making it perfect for AI in games.

Step 4: Choose the Right Platform. Aside from the data required to train your AI model, you must select the appropriate platform for your needs. You can choose an in-house or cloud framework. What is the primary difference between these frameworks? The cloud enables organizations to experiment and expand when projects enter production and demand rises by allowing for faster training and deployment of ML models.

✓ **Cloud frameworks**

You can train and deploy your models more quickly with an ML-as-a-service platform, also known as cloud ML. Models can be built and deployed using IDEs, Jupiter Notebooks, and other graphical user interfaces.

✓ **In-house frameworks**

Scikit, TensorFlow, and Pytorch are some of the options available. These are the most commonly used for developing models internally.

Step 5: Create and Select an Algorithm. When you tell the computer what to do, you also have to specify how it will do it. That's where computer algorithms come in. Algorithms are mathematical instructions. It is vital to develop prediction or classification machine learning algorithms so that the AI model can learn from the dataset.

There are numerous algorithms for various types of activities. Depending on the problem, you could utilize a combination of each:

✓ **Neural Networks:** Inspired by the human brain, these algorithms excel at dealing with complicated patterns and massive datasets, such as those found in healthcare systems, to improve decision-making and efficiency.

✓ **Clustering Algorithms:** These are used to group things so that they are more similar to one another than to those in other groups. This could be beneficial for segmenting patient kinds and optimizing resource allocation.

✓ **Decision Tree Algorithms:** These algorithms make decisions based on a set of rules. For example, they could select the optimum scheduling technique based on the type of appointment and time of day.

✓ **Classification Algorithms:** These algorithms arrange data into predetermined categories. For example, in a healthcare context, patients may be classified based on their likelihood of skipping appointments, allowing the system to change schedules accordingly.

✓ **Predictive Algorithms:** These use historical data to forecast future outcomes. To lower patient wait times, for example, a predictive algorithm could examine previous appointment durations and forecast future demand.

Step 6: Train the algorithms.

Moving on with the AI creation process, you must train the algorithm with the obtained data.

During the training process, the algorithm should be optimized to produce a high-accuracy AI model. However, you may require more data to improve the accuracy of your model.

Model correctness is the most important step to take. As a result, you must define model correctness by specifying a minimum acceptable level.

For example, a social networking firm aiming to remove false accounts can assign each account a "fraud score" ranging from 0 to 1. After some research, the team can opt to forward any accounts with a score of more than 0.9 to the fraud team.

Step 7: Deploy and monitor.

Finally, once you've created a sustainable and self-sufficient solution, it's time to implement it. By monitoring your models after deployment, you can ensure they continue to perform well. Don't forget to regularly check the operation.

Chapter 7

Tips for Learning AI.

Starting the path to study AI might be frightening, but taking a systematic approach can help to plan and manage the process more efficiently. Here are five stages to help you navigate your AI learning journey:

1. **Keep iterating.**

   Artificial intelligence is a rapidly expanding field. Once you've mastered the fundamentals, you should continue to learn and improve your talents. Follow AI blogs, read research papers, take advanced classes, and continually look for new ways to push oneself. This iterative method will take you from novice to expert.

   Remember that learning AI is both tough and rewarding. Don't be disheartened if you face challenges along the way; they're all part of the learning process. Keep your end objective in mind and keep focused on your trip.

2. **Join a community.**
   Join AI communities, both online and off. Participating in forums such as Stack Overflow or GitHub, joining AI groups, receiving LinkedIn newsletters, and attending AI events and conferences can all provide great learning opportunities.

   Joining communities allows you to remain up to date on the newest trends, ask for help when you get stuck, and network with other AI aficionados.

3. **Start learning.**
   Once you've decided on a focus, it's time to begin learning. The learning materials listed in the skills section, as well as the AI learning plan above, are good places to start. Remember: mastering AI is a marathon, not a sprint. Take your time understanding each topic before moving on to the next one.

4. **Apply your abilities to tasks.**

There is no better way to learn than via doing. Applying the skills, you learn in real-world projects strengthens your understanding and provides you with practical experience that can help you build your portfolio. This might be as basic as building a machine learning model to forecast housing values or as complex as designing a deep learning model for picture recognition. We've included some sample projects throughout this tutorial.

5. **Select your focus.**

Begin by determining where to direct your efforts based on your career objectives. In this article, we will go over the various AI occupations in further detail; each role has a particular focus and demands a specific skill set.

For example, if you want to work as a data scientist or machine learning engineer, you should study programming, data science, and various machine learning algorithms. Your goal here is to become adept in applying AI principles to real-world challenges.

Alternatively, if you're interested in a research career, you should learn more about the theory of AI and machine learning. You will need a thorough understanding of mathematics, statistics, and theoretical computer science.

This is not a hard difference; rather, it serves as a beginning point for determining where to focus your initial efforts.

Conclusion

Learning artificial intelligence is a rewarding quest that leads to a world of cutting-edge technologies and interesting employment options.

The information and experience obtained from this method extend beyond textbooks and seminars.

It entails a continuous cycle of learning, application, experimentation, and improvement. Taking a hands-on approach, particularly through courses and AI projects, accelerates learning while also cultivating crucial problem-solving, critical thinking, and creativity abilities.

www.ingramcontent.com/pod-product-compliance
Lightning Source LLC
La Vergne TN
LVHW051624050326
832903LV00033B/4650